ESSENTIAL
3-INGREDIENT
COCKTAILS

· ESSENTIAL ·
3-INGREDIENT
COCKTAILS

75 CLASSIC
AND CONTEMPORARY DRINKS
TO MAKE AT HOME

AMY TRAYNOR

ROCKRIDGE
PRESS

Interior and Cover Designer: Antonio Valverde
Art Producer: Janice Ackerman
Editor: Gurvinder Singh Gandu
Production Editor: Emily Sheehan

Photography: © 2020 Ted & Chelsea Cavanaugh.
Illustration: © 2020 Coen Pohl.

ISBN: Print 978-1-64611-859-5 | eBook 978-1-64611-860-1

R0

To my husband, Jeff, and his liver,
for their dedication to my craft.

CONTENTS

RASPBERRY BOURBON SOUR, PAGE 53

INTRODUCTION

There's something special about the number three. It represents beauty, harmony, completion . . . and simplicity. Not surprisingly, some of the most popular and classic cocktails are composed of just three ingredients. The old-fashioned, martini, Negroni, margarita, and gin and tonic are all 3-ingredient drinks, each perfectly balanced in its own way.

As a cocktail enthusiast for the past 10+ years, I know how daunting it can be to dip your toe into the world of home cocktail crafting. It took me many years of making and drinking subpar cocktails to realize that there are a lot of very simple cocktail recipes out there that are both great-tasting and feasible for the casual home bartender.

One of the biggest revelations in my home bartending struggle came when my mother shared with me that she'd read about a perfect cocktail "formula." She said that if you use the right proportions, you could make a great cocktail with pretty much any spirit, some simple syrup, and either lemon or lime juice. She made me a classic daiquiri as an example, and it was like drinking liquid sunshine. Up until that point, I'd been just blindly trying one old-fashioned or whiskey sour recipe after another, wondering why they were all so different, and why most didn't seem very balanced. For the first time, I understood the balancing act of basic 3-ingredient sour-style cocktails, such as the daiquiri and the margarita. From that moment, my interest took off, and over the course of a few years and a whole lot of cocktails, it led me to my current role as a professional cocktail recipe developer and blogger.

It is entirely possible to make fantastic cocktails from the comfort of your home, without years of experience or lots of fancy equipment and ingredients. All you need is a little bit of time to learn the tools of the trade, a few bottles that interest and excite you, and these 75 tried-and-tested recipes. Once you dive into this collection of easy-to-make, properly balanced cocktails, you'll develop a deeper understanding of what connects the core recipe templates that create great cocktails.

It's my hope that this book will help and inspire anyone with an interest in making drinks at home, whether you already have an impressive home bar setup or you just bought your first shaker. I'm here to simplify what wasn't very simple for me when I was getting started and to share some helpful tips I've learned along the way. The recipes are categorized by spirit to make it easy to start mixing with your favorite liquors right away. First, we'll talk tools and techniques. Then we'll jump right into the drinks, which are a carefully selected collection of vintage cocktails, modern classics, and a few recipes of my own. I hope these pages will become a trusted sidekick on your home mixology journey and inspire you to shake up some cocktail creations of your own!

PART ONE

THE HOME BAR ESSENTIALS

Having the right tools and ingredients on hand will make crafting a delicious cocktail at home even quicker and easier. The most important element of a well-made cocktail is high-quality ingredients, but that doesn't mean you have to break the bank at the liquor store. Use fresh juices and pick up some mid-range bottles and a few key tools, and your drinks will rival the best bars in town.

In this section, we'll cover the ingredients of a well-stocked home bar, the tools you need and how to use them, and the importance of choosing the right glassware. The section also includes some helpful tips, such as how to choose the best-tasting limes, how long to shake a cocktail, and how to make clear ice at home. Once you've mastered a few easy techniques, you can create all 75 recipes in this book with confidence.

CHAPTER 1

BAR TOOLS & EQUIPMENT

The right tools really make all the difference when creating any cocktail, whether at home or behind the neighborhood bar. When you're just getting started, bar tools can seem a little intimidating, but fear not—I'm going to walk you through them one by one, explaining exactly what each tool is for and how it's used. Lucky for us, professional bartenders have had a couple hundred years to develop some pretty efficient tools of the trade, making life for a home mixologist that much easier.

A well-made cocktail is a blend of art and science. Let's jump into the science component first, then we'll put our skills to use with the recipes.

ESSENTIAL TOOLS

BARSPOON: A barspoon is essentially a shallow teaspoon with a long, twisted handle. Barspoons make stirring cocktails a breeze because the small spoon gently holds the ice while you spin the ingredients in the glass. They are also handy for measuring small quantities of ingredients, such as strong liqueurs. Ever wonder why the handle is twisted? It's to allow liquids to slide smoothly down the handle when layering them in a glass, such as for layered shots or for cocktails like the White Russian (page 75).

CITRUS REAMER/PRESS: My citrus press is my right-hand man. A simple elbow design lets you extract fresh juices from lemons and limes with very little effort. Freshly squeezed citrus juice is critical to delicious cocktails, and this piece of equipment makes it a breeze.

JIGGER: A jigger allows you to accurately measure the liquid you're adding to your cocktail. Look for one that has multiple measuring lines, from ½ ounce (¼ ounce is even better) up to 2 ounces. Jiggers are essential for creating consistent, balanced, and reproduceable cocktails.

LARGE ICE CUBE MOLDS: If you enjoy spirit-forward cocktails such as the old-fashioned or Negroni, invest in some large ice cube molds. Larger ice melts more slowly, which means less dilution and a better-tasting cocktail. If you like, you can take it a step further by creating your own custom-cut clear ice, right from the comfort of your kitchen (page 26).

MICROPLANE: A microplane is the ideal tool for grating both citrus zest and fresh spice garnishes like nutmeg. Compared to its ground form, freshly grated nutmeg is much more fragrant, so it makes a noticeable difference in cocktails like the Brandy Alexander (page 120).

MUDDLER: A muddler is a long, blunt-ended tool made of wood or metal that allows you to extract juices and oils from fruits and herbs by pressing down on them firmly. Choose a simple wooden one without any bells or whistles and you'll save yourself a headache when it's time to clean up.

SHAKER: Cocktail shakers consist of two- or three-piece setups that allow you to vigorously combine and chill ingredients. Three-piece, Cobbler-style shakers are a common choice for home bartenders because the strainer is built-in. Boston- and French-style shakers are two-piece units that

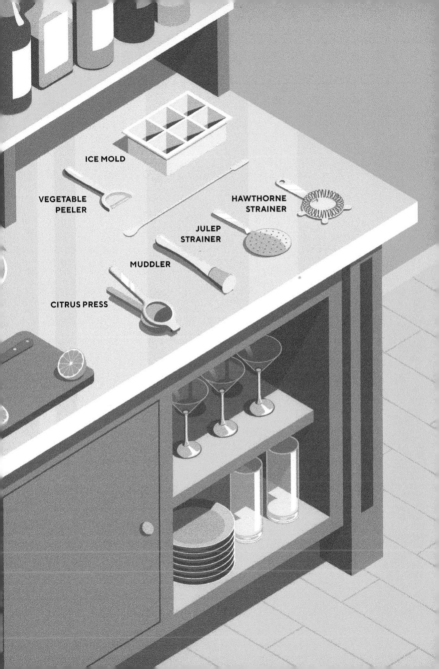

ICE MOLD

VEGETABLE
PEELER

HAWTHORNE
STRAINER

JULEP
STRAINER

MUDDLER

CITRUS PRESS

require the addition of a strainer. My recommendation: Pick up an inexpensive classic Boston shaker with a metal tin and a glass. This is the most economical option for a beginner because you can use both pieces for a shaken cocktail and the mixing glass for stirred cocktails.

TIP: Not sure how long to shake a cocktail? Twelve seconds of vigorous shaking is usually enough to fully chill and emulsify the ingredients.

STRAINER: A strainer's purpose is to transfer the cocktail from shaker to glass, while leaving the ice behind. There are two primary types of cocktail strainers: the Hawthorne and the julep. Hawthorne strainers are rounded and feature a coiled spring along the edge that does the straining. Julep strainers look like large metal slotted spoons and are most commonly used for straining stirred cocktails. If you're looking for one all-purpose strainer, choose a Hawthorne.

TIP: If you enjoy cocktails that involve muddling ingredients, pick up an inexpensive fine-mesh strainer so that you can fine-strain, or "double strain," your cocktail.

VEGETABLE PEELER: A Y-shaped vegetable peeler holds a prominent place in my home bar for removing citrus peels. Yes, you can remove citrus peels with a sharp knife, but vegetable peelers make the job much safer, easier, and quicker.

GLASSWARE

Glassware can be one of the most fun and interesting elements of your home bar. Although bar tools provide some of the science component of craft cocktails, glassware can add to the artistic side of things, increasing visual appeal and enhancing the drinking experience. There are many different glass styles to choose from, but you don't have to own them all to enjoy your drinks at home. These are the glasses you'll need most often:

 COUPE: A coupe is a rounded, shallow, stemmed glass that was originally designed for serving Champagne (which is why it is also known as a Champagne saucer). Use of a coupe for drinking Champagne eventually fell out of favor, but it was destined for bigger things, becoming the primary vessel for some of the world's greatest cocktails served "up." Examples of cocktails served in coupe glasses include the daiquiri, the gimlet, and the Brown Derby.

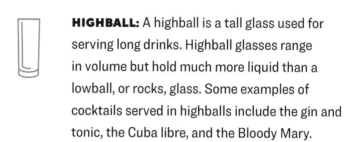

HIGHBALL: A highball is a tall glass used for serving long drinks. Highball glasses range in volume but hold much more liquid than a lowball, or rocks, glass. Some examples of cocktails served in highballs include the gin and tonic, the Cuba libre, and the Bloody Mary.

JULEP CUP: A julep cup is a silver cup traditionally used for serving mint juleps. The metal, combined with crushed ice, keeps the drink very cold and gives it a beautiful presentation.

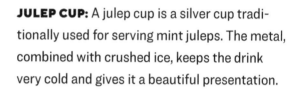

MARTINI GLASS: The martini glass, also sometimes just called a cocktail glass, is known for its iconic conical bowl. Its sleek design has made it the vessel of choice not just for the martini but also for many other cocktails, including the Manhattan, the brandy Alexander, and the Grasshopper.

MULE MUG: This is a copper mug made for serving Moscow mules. Like the julep cup, a mule mug's purpose is to keep the drink frosty and add visual appeal.

ROCKS GLASS: The rocks, old-fashioned, or lowball glass is a short, often heavy-bottomed glass made for drinking spirits neat or over ice as well as for shorter cocktails. In addition to the old-fashioned, other cocktails served in a rocks glass include the Negroni, the gold rush, and the whiskey sour.

TIP: If you want to add to your glassware collection without spending a fortune, check out local thrift shops. The majority of my collection consists of beautiful vintage pieces that I scored for just $1 each.

CHAPTER 2

THE COMPONENTS OF 3-INGREDIENT COCKTAILS

The beauty of the 3-ingredient cocktail is simplicity. There are just enough ingredients for creating balance and layered flavor, but nothing extra or unnecessary. Quality ingredients are key to any cocktail, but that's especially true when you're only working with a few of them. The most common 3-ingredient cocktails feature the following elements: a spirit, a sweetener of some kind, and either a sour or bitter ingredient. Not every 3-ingredient cocktail follows this rule, but this popular template plays out over and over in some of the most timeless drinks.

One of the joys of making cocktails at home is that once you understand some basic recipe formulas, you can start to substitute your own ingredients in classic recipes to create delicious custom drinks.

SPIRITS

Let's look at the different types of spirits that this book's recipes will explore. Liquors are the star ingredient in cocktails, so you'll want to make sure you're using high-quality bottles. We'll talk a bit about what makes each spirit unique, what each spirit tastes like, and some product recommendations for getting started.

WHISKEY

Whiskey is one of the world's oldest spirits, and from the early days, it has captivated drinkers with its warmth and toasted flavors. Whiskey is made from fermented cereal grains such as corn, rye, wheat, and barley. Let's talk more about the two primary whiskeys featured in this book: bourbon and rye.

Bourbon

Bourbon is a whiskey made according to legal requirements in the United States. One of the primary rules for bourbon is that the "mash bill," or the grains used in fermentation, be at least 51 percent corn. Corn gives bourbon its characteristic sweetness, which can translate to notes of vanilla, caramel, and dried fruit after it's been aged. Bourbon must be aged in new oak barrels for a minimum of two years. I haven't met a bourbon I didn't like, but some great bottles to get started with are Bulleit, Woodford Reserve, and Knob Creek.

Rye

In the United States, "rye whiskey" refers to a whiskey made with a mash bill of at least 51 percent rye. Rye imparts a spicy flavor and makes for a much drier, less sweet whiskey. Both bourbon and rye may share similar flavors and aromas, such as honey, leather, nuts, or oak, but rye whiskeys also tend to possess spicier flavors, such as black pepper, clove, or cinnamon. Some great ryes include Redemption, Rittenhouse, Sazerac, and Whistle Pig.

GIN

With its crisp flavor and versatility showcased in a wide range of cocktails, gin is one of the most popular spirits in America today. Gin is a clear spirit that is flavored with a variety of botanicals, with juniper berries being the most prominent. London dry is one of the most common and traditional types of gin, with all flavoring being added via natural botanicals during distillation. In some ways, this distillation-added flavoring is really what distinguishes gin from vodka. Today, there are innumerable gins to choose from, some with wildly different flavors due to the flexible labeling requirements for the category. If you're looking for classic gin flavor, choose brands like Bombay, Tanqueray, Plymouth, or The Botanist.

VODKA

Vodka is the most popular type of liquor in the world and, not coincidentally, the most neutral-tasting. Vodka first appeared centuries ago in Russia and Poland. Today, it is made primarily from potatoes, cereal grains, or fruit. A great benefit of creating cocktails with vodka is its ability to fortify other flavors and allow them to become the focus of the drink. Vodka is not truly tasteless, but it is subtly flavored due to the multiple filtration processes that most producers use. When purchasing vodka, look for high-quality brands such as Absolut, Tito's Handmade, or Grey Goose for the best flavor and smoothness.

RUM

Rum is a category of spirits made from fermented sugar-cane molasses or juice. Being made with sugar, rums are naturally sweet, with flavors ranging widely from grassy to caramelized, depending on the style and age. Unlike other types of liquors, rums can be made using a variety of production methods. As a result, rums from different distillers can be quite different, even within the same country or region. Some of the most popular rums come from Jamaica, Barbados, Puerto Rico, Venezuela, and Cuba.

White rums

White rums are aged briefly and tend to have lighter, brighter flavors and a characteristic sweetness. They are milder and more light-bodied than dark rums, making them perfect for light and refreshing cocktails. There are many quality white rums on the market beyond the ever-popular Bacardi Superior. If you're looking to try something different and noteworthy, I recommend Brugal Especial Extra Dry, Diplomático Planas, or Havana Club Añejo 3 Años.

Dark rums vary greatly depending on the region they're from, their age, and how they are produced. Aged rums are treasure troves of deeper, more complex flavors, such as tropical fruit, vanilla, and spice. I recommend starting with approachable yet flavorful high-quality aged rums from Jamaica and Barbados, such as Plantation, Appleton Estate, and Mount Gay.

TEQUILA

Tequila is a type of mezcal produced within specific regions of Mexico using only blue agave plants. The agaves are harvested at peak ripeness and trimmed of their long stalks. Then the cores, or piñas, are slowly cooked to break down the plant's sugars. The extracted juices from the piñas are fermented and distilled at least twice. Tequila flavors range from fruity to earthy to oaky, depending on where they're made and how long they're aged. Blanco (unaged) and reposado (aged up to one year) tequilas are great in a variety of cocktails. Brands I recommend include Tres Agaves, Patrón, and Espolon.

MEZCAL

Mezcal is a spirit native to Mexico that may be made from any type of agave plant. Mezcal has a distinct smoky flavor because the agave piñas are roasted in underground pits for a few days before the juices are extracted for fermentation. Mezcal flavors range from fruity to vegetal, with varying degrees of smokiness. A few bottles to try at home are Del Maguey Vida, Montelobos, and Mezcal El Silencio.

LIQUEURS AND FORTIFIED WINES

Liqueurs and fortified wines add much of the flavor and character to our 3-ingredient cocktails. These secondary alcohols either modify the flavor of the main spirit or create a new dimension of flavor, often while adding sweetness. Although all liqueurs are sweetened to some degree, the alcohol content can vary widely, from relatively weak Aperol at 11 percent alcohol by volume (ABV) to the very potent green Chartreuse at 55 percent ABV.

APEROL

Aperol is a mild, bittersweet orange-flavored liqueur from Italy. Although it is often compared with Campari, it is significantly less bitter, with a pronounced orange flavor that is reminiscent of tangerine. Aperol is perhaps best known for its role in the famous Aperol Spritz (page 134), a low ABV 3-ingredient cocktail that's perfect for afternoon sipping.

COINTREAU

Cointreau is a premium orange-flavored liqueur (also called triple sec) from France. Cointreau has a clean, crisp orange flavor that brings several classic cocktails to life. The Margarita (page 104), the Sidecar (page 121), and the Lemon Drop (page 84) are examples of 3-ingredient cocktails that feature Cointreau for its flavor and sweetness.

CHARTREUSE

Chartreuse is a powerful herbal liqueur famously made by French monks according to a secret recipe. Today, there are both green and yellow versions of Chartreuse, the latter being a slightly milder and less potent liqueur. Chartreuse's boldly herbaceous flavor is present in several classic cocktails, including the gin-based cocktail the Alaska (page 66).

CRÈME DE CACAO

This chocolate-flavored liqueur adds decadence to cocktails like the classic Brandy Alexander (page 120). Crème de cacao comes in white (clear) or dark (brown) varieties, depending on how you want the final cocktail to look. I highly recommend investing in a high-quality bottle, such as Tempus Fugit's Crème de Cacao a la Vanille.

CRÈME DE MENTHE

The sweet mint flavor and bright green color of crème de menthe makes it a key ingredient in the beloved dessert cocktail the Grasshopper (page 130). It is also available in a clear variety.

THE COMPONENTS OF 3-INGREDIENT COCKTAILS

ICE MATTERS

Understanding and using high-quality ice will improve your home bartending exponentially. Although often overlooked, the ice that you use to make and serve your drinks has a big impact on the taste of the final drink. It's important to be consistent and use fresh ice straight from the freezer, rather than half-melted ice from a bucket on the counter. Melting ice, or "wet" ice, will melt more quickly in the cocktail shaker or glass, causing too much dilution. Many home mixologists find it convenient to make large cubes using silicone molds. Large cubes dissolve more slowly, preventing the cocktail from getting too watered down. They're ideal for short, strong drinks such as the old-fashioned. Crushed ice is used in many cocktails to provide excess dilution and to make the drink extra chilled. Examples of cocktails that use crushed ice are the mint julep and the sherry cobbler.

Although not an absolute requirement for great-tasting cocktails, clear ice is the gold standard for flavor (it has fewer impurities) and is slow melting (it doesn't contain pockets of air bubbles like typical homemade ice). Don't be intimidated by making your own blocks of clear ice at home. It can be accomplished even with limited freezer space. Making and cutting your own custom clear ice takes your home bartending game and your drink-making skills to the next level, with truly handcrafted cocktails.

To make clear ice, all you'll need is a small, lunch-sized cooler, some water, and patience. Make sure the cooler is clean before you begin. Start by filling the cooler with room temperature water until it's about ¾ full. Place the cooler in the freezer and leave the lid open or propped partially open to allow air flow. The cold air in the freezer will chill the water from the top down, creating a layer of crystal-clear ice on top, and a pocket of air and impurities below. Leave the cooler in the freezer for 18 to 24 hours (the exact time will depend on how cold your freezer is). The ice is ready when there's a thick layer of ice on top and a visible pool or pocket of liquid water remaining below. It's okay to remove it a bit early—you'll just have a thinner slab of ice. If you leave it for too long, however, you'll end up with a block of ice that is clear on top and cloudy on the bottom. This is still okay, but you'll want to cut off the cloudy section.

Once you have a solid block of ice, allow the cooler to sit on the counter for about 20 minutes so that the ice thaws enough to slide out easily. Remove the ice from the cooler and drain any excess water. Transfer the ice block to a cutting board and let temper for an additional 20 minutes or so. By letting the ice melt just a bit, it will be easier to cut without shattering or splintering. Use a serrated knife to score the ice into the cube sizes you desire. Then you can use a larger knife and a mallet to gently tap the scored lines and easily break up the block. Store your custom-cut ice in freezer bags or plastic containers in the freezer.

If you want clear ice but you don't want to cut it yourself, you can opt for a product such as the Wintersmith Ice Chest, available on Amazon. This insulated chest works just like the above cooler method, but it has interior molds to easily create square or round ice, and it takes up considerably less freezer space.

KAHLUA

Kahlua is a popular coffee-flavored liqueur from Mexico. Made with coffee, rum, and vanilla, it has a smooth, well-rounded flavor that works well in many cocktails, from the Espresso Martini (page 76) to the White Russian (page 75).

ST-GERMAIN

St-Germain is an elderflower-flavored liqueur from France. Elderflower liqueur has a unique floral and fruity flavor that tastes sort of like lychees or pears. St-Germain has become a modern cocktail staple found in many recipes, such as the Elderflower Gimlet (page 68) and the Elderflower Spritz (page 135).

VERMOUTHS

Vermouths are fortified wines flavored with herbs and fruit. Vermouth can be made with red or white wines, and they come in sweet and dry varieties. Dry vermouth is best known for its role in the classic Martini (page 56), and sweet vermouth is an integral ingredient in many

3-ingredient cocktails, including the Manhattan
(page 43), the Negroni (page 62), and the Americano
(page 131).

CITRUS

Citrus plays a vital role in many 3-ingredient cocktails,
adding the sour or tart flavors that balance the main spirit
and sweetener. Limes, lemons, oranges, and grapefruits
should all be freshly squeezed for juice whenever possible.
Bottled or concentrated juices taste dramatically different
from fresh juices and have no place in cocktails! To pick the
best-tasting, juiciest lemons and limes, look for ones with
smooth, rather than bumpy, skin. When you gently squeeze
the fruit, it should give a little. Rock-hard lemons and limes
are much harder to extract juice from and will produce a lot
less juice overall.

SWEETENERS

Sweeteners are another key cocktail component. In addition to balancing the flavor of spirits or citrus juices,
sweeteners often add their own flavor to the cocktail. It's

very easy to make flavored simple syrups at home. For the recipes in this book, we'll use simple syrup, demerara syrup, honey syrups, herb syrups, fruit syrup, and even syrup made from flowers. Sugar cubes are used in classic cocktail preparations, although today it is more common to use liquid simple syrup in place of slow-to-dissolve cubes to ensure consistency. We'll also use a few easy-to-find store-bought syrups, including orgeat (almond syrup), grenadine, and agave syrups.

SIMPLE SYRUPS

SIMPLE SYRUP: Simple syrup is the very simple mix of equal parts water and sugar. There is really no need to use heat when making simple syrup; you can just stir until all the sugar has dissolved, which takes only a few minutes. If you're short on time, you can make it in less than a minute by using hot water and stirring briskly. A standard recipe is 1 cup of water to 1 cup of white sugar, although you can make as much or as little as you like. Store simple syrup sealed in a clean glass jar in the refrigerator. It will keep for about 2 to 3 weeks. You can add 1 ounce of vodka to help it stay fresh for a bit longer if you like.

DEMERARA SYRUP: The only difference between simple syrup and demerara syrup is the type of sugar being used. Demerara sugar is minimally processed and contains a small amount of molasses, giving it a distinctive caramel flavor. I find that this deeper flavor works beautifully in cocktails with aged spirits, such as whiskey and rum, and it is often my preferred sweetener in a classic old-fashioned. Demerara sugar and brown sugar are not the same, but you could substitute brown sugar in a pinch. To make demerara syrup, combine equal parts demerara sugar with warm or hot water. Stir until all the sugar has dissolved and store sealed in a clean glass jar in the refrigerator. Demerara syrup will keep for 2 to 3 weeks.

HONEY SYRUP: Honey syrup is just as easy to make as simple syrup. To make honey syrup, combine equal parts honey and water and stir until the honey has dissolved. Store sealed in a clean glass jar in the refrigerator for up to 2 weeks.

GINGER HONEY SYRUP: This is a simple honey syrup that's infused with fresh ginger. Combine 1 cup of honey, 1¼ cups of water, and ½ cup of peeled and chopped fresh ginger in a saucepan. Bring to a boil, then reduce to low heat and simmer until it has a strong ginger flavor, 15 to 20 minutes.

Because this syrup will cook for a relatively long time, I like to add a little extra water to account for what will boil off. Once the syrup is done, remove from heat and allow to cool. Strain out the ginger and store the syrup sealed in a clean glass jar in the refrigerator for up to 2 weeks.

MINT SYRUP: To make mint syrup, you infuse a simple syrup with mint leaves, as if making a cup of tea. I like to pour hot simple syrup over fresh mint, cover, let cool, and then strain out the leaves. This produces a richly flavored syrup by retaining as much of the plant's natural oils as possible, without overheating the herb. Start by measuring approximately 1 cup of mint leaves. If you have very large leaves, you can chop them into smaller pieces. Put the mint in a 2-cup glass measuring cup. Next, combine 1 cup of sugar with 1 cup of water in a small saucepan. Heat the mixture on medium heat, stirring frequently, until it begins to bubble. Remove from heat and pour over the mint leaves. Cover with plastic wrap and let sit until cooled. Once the syrup is cool, strain out the mint leaves and store the syrup sealed in a clean glass jar in the refrigerator for up to 2 weeks.

ROSEMARY SYRUP: Rosemary is a more robust herb than mint and can handle more heat. Combine 1 cup of sugar and 1 cup of water in a small saucepan. Heat on medium, stirring frequently, until the sugar has dissolved. Add 3 sprigs of rosemary to the pan, bring to a boil, then reduce heat and allow the syrup to simmer for 5 to 10 minutes, or until flavorful enough for you. Remove from heat, strain out the rosemary, and store the syrup sealed in a clean glass jar in the refrigerator. It will last up to 2 weeks.

HIBISCUS SYRUP: Hibiscus syrup is a wonderful way to add color and a sweet-tart floral flavor to cocktails. Dried hibiscus is readily available in bulk from natural food stores, and you can also find it in tea bags in most grocery stores. To make hibiscus syrup, begin by placing ½ cup of dried hibiscus flowers in a 2-cup glass measuring cup. Combine 1 cup of water and 1 cup of sugar in a small saucepan. Heat on medium, stirring frequently, until the sugar has dissolved. Remove from heat and pour the syrup over the hibiscus flowers. Stir to combine and let steep for at least 20 minutes. Strain out the hibiscus and store the syrup sealed in a clean glass jar in the refrigerator for up to 2 weeks.

BLACKBERRY SYRUP: Combine 1 cup of sugar and 1 cup of water in a small saucepan. Heat on medium, stirring frequently, until the sugar has dissolved. Add 2 cups of fresh blackberries to the pan, bring to a boil, then reduce heat and allow the syrup to simmer for 5 to 10 minutes, or until the fruit begins to break down. Remove from heat, strain out the blackberries, and store the syrup sealed in a clean glass jar in the refrigerator. Blackberry syrup will last up to 2 weeks.

TIP: This basic recipe can be used to make syrups from any kind of berry.

BITTERS

Bitters are like the salt and pepper of mixology. They can adjust the character of the drink or bring out flavors in the main spirit. Just a dash or two of these potently-flavored tinctures can dramatically transform the flavor of your final cocktail. Bitters are used in many cocktails, and they can also be a fun way to experiment with creating your own variations on classic recipes by making subtle adjustments. Angostura is one of the most well-known brands and is used in many timeless recipes. Angostura bitters are made with a secret blend of herbs and spices that includes gentian root as a bittering agent. Another classic brand of bitters is Peychaud's. Peychaud's bitters are bright red, with a somewhat fruity, spiced flavor that is milder than the very robust Angostura. Orange bitters are produced by many different brands, but all have a bright and crisp orange flavor that brings out citrusy flavors in gin and adds a light, fresh quality to a classic martini.

OTHER MIXERS

Other mixers we'll use in our 3-ingredient cocktails include cola, tonic water, ginger beer, ginger ale, grapefruit soda, Bloody Mary mix, and sparkling water. These mixers are ready to use, making delicious tall drinks quick and easy. I recommend choosing high-quality brands whenever possible, such as Fever-Tree and Q Mixers.

GARNISHES

Now that we've assembled our shaken or stirred 3-ingredient cocktail, the garnish is the finishing touch. For our purposes, garnishes aren't counted as one of our

3 ingredients. The word *garnish* literally means "a decoration," and one of its primary purposes is to enhance the beauty and visual appeal of your cocktail. It's said that we first drink with our eyes, and the appeal of a well-dressed drink can go a long way toward its enjoyment. Citrus peel garnishes serve yet another purpose, as their expressed oils alter the final flavor of the cocktail, sometimes dramatically. Fragrant botanical garnishes, such as a sprig of mint, are employed because their aroma alters the drink experience. (We do a lot of our tasting through our sense of smell, after all.) Although they won't taste exactly the same, it is entirely possible to still enjoy any of the recipes in this book without a garnish. Here are some of the common garnishes we'll be using:

CITRUS PEEL TWIST: To make a citrus peel twist, use a Y-peeler or a sharp paring knife to carefully remove a strip of the rind, being careful not to remove too much of the white pith, which can add a bitter taste. To express the citrus oils over your cocktail, hold the peel facing the surface of the drink and squeeze, bending the edges of the peel backward. You'll see a fine mist of oils spray from the peel and onto the surface of the cocktail. Next, rub the peel along the edge of the glass and drop it into the drink.

CITRUS WHEELS, SLICES, AND WEDGES: Pieces of citrus fruit add a bit of fresh flavor, aroma, and visual flair to many cocktails. A *wheel* refers to a whole round cut of citrus, sliced from the middle of the fruit, in between the two ends. A *slice* usually refers to half of a wheel. To create citrus wedges, cut both ends off the fruit. Cut the fruit in half, lengthwise, then place each side flat and cut lengthwise, making about four wedges from each half.

CHERRIES: Cocktail cherries add a sweet treat to the end of the drinking experience. You can choose maraschino cherries or brandied cherries, but opt for high-quality, undyed cherries for the best flavor. Luxardo Maraschino cherries are my top choice for cocktails like the Manhattan and whiskey sour.

OLIVES: The green olive is a classic martini and Bloody Mary garnish, and its saltiness adds just the right touch to savory cocktails. Depending on your cocktail and your preferences, you can choose olives stuffed with pimento, blue cheese, or even jalapeño pepper.

NUTMEG: Freshly grated nutmeg is a classic cocktail garnish that adds a lovely aromatic layer to drinks like the brandy Alexander. I like to buy whole nutmeg and grate with a microplane for the freshest flavor, but you could sprinkle on powdered nutmeg in a pinch.

PART TWO

3-INGREDIENT COCKTAILS

Now it's time to dive into the 3-ingredient cocktails. The following recipes are a mix of time-honored classics, modern mainstays, and a few recipes of my own creation. For convenience, the recipes in the first five chapters are categorized by spirit. The final chapter includes 20 bonus recipes made with a variety of other spirits and wines including Cognac, Champagne, and vermouth. Feel free to flip from chapter to chapter depending on the spirits you personally prefer. In chapter 8, there are some recipes to help you get to know some other, less common spirits such as Calvados and aquavit, as well as a few classic lower-ABV options for those days when you want a lighter drink.

OLD-FASHIONED, PAGE 42

WHISKEY

OLD-FASHIONED

2 ounces bourbon or
rye whiskey

¼ ounce simple
syrup (see page 30)

2 dashes
Angostura bitters

Orange twist,
for garnish

The old-fashioned is the original cocktail. This simple blend of spirit, sweetener, and bitters is both timeless and delicious. It's an excellent way to first taste a new bottle of any aged spirit, especially bourbon or rye whiskey. Although there are varying claims about where and when the old-fashioned was born, it first appeared in the 1800s, when it was referred to as "bittered sling."

INSTRUCTIONS:

Combine the whiskey, syrup, and bitters in a mixing glass. Fill ¾ of the glass with ice. Stir until chilled, about 30 seconds. Strain the drink into a rocks glass filled with ice (or one large cube). Garnish with an expressed orange twist.

ESSENTIAL 3-INGREDIENT COCKTAILS

MANHATTAN

2 ounces
rye whiskey

1 ounce sweet
vermouth

2 dashes
orange bitters

Cocktail cherry,
for garnish

The Manhattan is a classic whiskey cocktail with mysterious origins and many tales regarding its invention, dating back to at least 1882 when it was first mentioned in a New York newspaper. A true whiskey lover's cocktail, it has just enough sweetness and complexity to open up the flavor of the rye.

INSTRUCTIONS:

Combine the whiskey, vermouth, and bitters in a mixing glass. Fill ¾ of the glass with ice. Stir until chilled, about 30 seconds. Strain the drink into a coupe or martini glass and garnish with a high-quality cocktail cherry.

BOULEVARDIER

1 ounce bourbon or
rye whiskey

1 ounce Campari

1 ounce sweet
vermouth

Orange twist,
for garnish

The boulevardier is a variation on the classic gin cocktail the Negroni (page 62) and is potent, rich, and bittersweet. Though they are often made with bourbon, I prefer my boulevardiers with spicier rye whiskey. This warming cocktail is the perfect winter sip to enjoy by a roaring fire after a long day.

INSTRUCTIONS:

Combine the whiskey, Campari, and vermouth in a mixing glass. Fill ¾ of the glass with ice. Stir until chilled, about 30 seconds. Strain the drink into a rocks glass filled with ice (or one large cube). Garnish with an expressed orange twist.

WHISKEY SOUR

2 ounces bourbon or
rye whiskey

¾ ounce simple
syrup (see page 30)

¾ ounce lemon juice

Orange slice,
for garnish

Cocktail cherry,
for garnish

The whiskey sour has been a popular way to enjoy whiskey since at least the late 1800s. There are many variations, including the addition of egg whites, but this basic recipe is a great place to start. You can use any type of whiskey in this delicious sweet-and-sour cocktail.

INSTRUCTIONS:

Combine the whiskey, syrup, and lemon juice in a cocktail shaker. Fill ¾ of the shaker with ice. Shake until chilled, about 12 seconds. Strain the drink into a rocks glass filled with ice and garnish with an orange slice and a high-quality cocktail cherry.

THE ORIGINS OF WHISKEY

Like trying to recall details of an evening when too much whis-key was consumed, the history of the spirit is a bit hazy. There are many stories about the origin of whiskey, but exactly where and when it was born remains a mystery. What we do know is that distillation appears to have arrived in Ireland sometime around the 11th century. By the late 15th century, whiskey production was underway in both Scotland and Ireland. Which country actually first produced whiskey is a hotly debated topic, but thankfully it arrived in America in the 1700s, birthing the rye- and corn-based whiskeys we've come to enjoy today.

The first commercial American whiskey distillery was founded in 1783 by Evan Williams.

It's said that rye whiskey was accidentally invented when Scotch-Irish settlers in the United States started making whiskey with the rye that grew abundantly in their new homeland. Because of the long shipping times, it was sometimes up to two years before the whiskey reached its destination. This accidental aging resulted in a new spirit that quickly gained popularity. For a long time, rye was the most popular whiskey in America, before bourbon took center stage. Perhaps the most famous distiller of rye whiskey was President George Washington, running one of the largest operations of the late 18th century.

Although produced since the late 1700s, bourbon wasn't officially labeled as such until 1840. Numerous legends surround the origin of the name, with the most popular claiming Jacob Spears was the first to coin the term. Elijah Craig is another key player in the history of bourbon, and he's often credited as the first to age corn whiskey in charred oak barrels. Prohibition and World War II drastically changed the landscape of American whiskey production, yet whiskey's popularity never wavered. Bourbon was officially declared a distinct American product by Congress in 1964, and, for the first time, a legal definition of its production was put in place. Today, both rye and bourbon are more popular than ever, enjoying renewed interest from a whole new generation of drinkers.

MINT JULEP

10 mint leaves

¼ ounce simple
syrup (see page 30)

2 ounces bourbon

Mint sprig,
for garnish

The mint julep originated in America and has become a staple of Southern summer festivities, most notably the Kentucky Derby. As early as the 1600s, juleps with varying herbs were prescribed as a type of medicine. Traditionally, they're prepared and served in silver julep cups, but a rocks glass will do in a pinch.

INSTRUCTIONS:

Place the mint leaves and the syrup in a julep cup or rocks glass. With a muddler, gently press on the mint leaves a few times to release their oils. Be careful not to overmuddle, as it can cause the mint to taste bitter. Add the bourbon and fill the cup with crushed ice. With a barspoon, stir until the cup frosts over. Top with more crushed ice and garnish with a sprig of mint.

GOLD RUSH

2 ounces bourbon

¾ ounce honey
syrup (see page 31)

¾ ounce lemon juice

The gold rush is one of many modern classics to originate at the famous New York City bar Milk & Honey. Invented by T. J. Siegal, the gold rush uses honey syrup instead of simple syrup for a rich variation on the classic whiskey sour.

INSTRUCTIONS:

Combine the bourbon, syrup, and lemon juice in a cocktail shaker. Fill ¾ of the shaker with ice. Shake until chilled, about 12 seconds. Strain the drink into a rocks glass filled with ice (or one large cube).

BROWN DERBY

1½ ounces bourbon

¾ ounce
grapefruit juice

¾ ounce honey
syrup (see page 31)

Grapefruit twist,
for garnish

The Brown Derby is a surprisingly refreshing bourbon cocktail made with grapefruit and honey. Invented at the trendy Vendôme Club in Los Angeles in the 1930s, the Brown Derby was named for a nearby diner. While it can be enjoyed any time you like, the Brown Derby is often considered a brunch cocktail.

INSTRUCTIONS:

Combine the bourbon, grapefruit juice, and syrup in a cocktail shaker. Fill ¾ of the shaker with ice. Shake until chilled, about 12 seconds. Strain the drink into a coupe glass and garnish with a grapefruit twist.

ESSENTIAL 3-INGREDIENT COCKTAILS

HOT TODDY

1½ ounces bourbon
or rye whiskey

½ ounce lemon juice

½ ounce honey
syrup (see page 31)

Cinnamon stick,
for garnish

3 cloves,
for garnish

Lemon wheel,
for garnish

There's no winter cocktail cozier than a spiced hot toddy. I like to use bourbon, but you can use any whiskey you prefer. Once touted as a cure-all, the hot toddy might not actually cure your cold, but it is undoubtedly one of the most soothing cocktails when you're under the weather. Hot toddies are easy to customize by garnishing with different spices, such as cinnamon, cloves, and star anise.

INSTRUCTIONS:

Put the whiskey, lemon juice, and syrup in an 8-ounce heatproof mug. Fill the mug with hot water and gently stir with a cinnamon stick. Insert the cloves into a lemon wheel and drop it into the mug.

WHISKEY BUCK

1½ ounces bourbon
or rye whiskey

½ ounce lime juice

6 ounces
ginger beer

Lime wedge,
for garnish

The whiskey buck, while lesser known, is closely related to the Dark Skies (page 91) and the Moscow Mule (page 74). Bucks are a category of cocktails dating back to the late 1800s that combine spirit with citrus and ginger beer. This easy-to-make, minimal-prep, crowd-pleasing recipe is a great choice for parties.

INSTRUCTIONS:

Fill a mule mug or highball glass with ice. Add the whiskey and lime juice and stir to chill. Top with the chilled ginger beer and garnish with a lime wedge.

ESSENTIAL 3-INGREDIENT COCKTAILS

RASPBERRY BOURBON SOUR

2 ounces bourbon

¾ ounce lemon juice

This tasty variation on a whiskey sour was inspired by the famous modern gin cocktail the Cosmonaut (page 65). I've swapped out the gin for bourbon in this equally delicious yet more richly flavored cocktail. Raspberry jam emphasizes the natural sweetness of the bourbon while tempering the acidity of the lemon juice.

INSTRUCTIONS:

Combine the bourbon, lemon juice, and jam in a cocktail shaker. Fill ¾ of the shaker with ice. Shake until chilled, about 12 seconds. Fine strain the drink into a coupe glass and garnish with a raspberry.

1 teaspoon
raspberry jam

Raspberry,
for garnish

ELDERFLOWER GIMLET, PAGE 68

GIN

MARTINI

2½ ounces gin

½ ounce dry vermouth

2 dashes orange bitters

Lemon twist, for garnish

The classic gin martini is perhaps the most iconic of all cocktails. The simple blend of crisp gin, herbaceous dry vermouth, and orange bitters has become popular around the world since its invention around the early 1900s. The history of the martini is unclear, although most agree that it likely evolved from the classic Martinez.

INSTRUCTIONS:

Combine the gin, vermouth, and bitters in a mixing glass. Fill ¾ of the glass with ice. Stir until chilled, about 30 seconds. Strain the drink into a martini glass and garnish with an expressed lemon twist.

ESSENTIAL 3-INGREDIENT COCKTAILS

DIRTY MARTINI

2½ ounces gin

½ ounce dry vermouth

1 barspoon green olive brine

3 green olives, for garnish

The dirty martini is a martini variation that replaces bitters with a few dashes of olive brine. The first dirty martini was made more than 100 years ago when a bartender decided to muddle the olive garnish into the drink. Although it's long been criticized by martini purists, the popularity of this salty, savory cocktail endures. Fun fact: Add more than a teaspoon of olive brine, and you've got yourself a filthy martini.

INSTRUCTIONS:

Combine the gin, vermouth, and olive brine in a mixing glass. Fill ¾ of the glass with ice. Stir until chilled, about 30 seconds. Strain the drink into a martini glass and garnish with three olives on a cocktail pick.

PERFECT MARTINI

1½ ounces gin

¾ ounce dry
vermouth

¾ ounce sweet
vermouth

Orange twist,
for garnish

Rather than referring to an ideal recipe, "perfect" cocktails are those containing equal measures of sweet and dry vermouth. The result is a slightly sweet martini variation that's satisfying and somewhat less potent than a classic martini. I enjoy mine with flavorful vermouths such as Noilly Prat dry vermouth and Carpano Antica Formula sweet vermouth.

INSTRUCTIONS:

Combine the gin and vermouths in a mixing glass. Fill ¾ of the glass with ice. Stir until chilled, about 30 seconds. Strain the drink into a martini glass and garnish with an expressed orange twist.

ESSENTIAL 3-INGREDIENT COCKTAILS

GIN AND TONIC

2 ounces gin

½ ounce lime juice

4 to 6 ounces
tonic water

Lime wedge,
for garnish

The gin and tonic was one of the earliest gin cocktails to gain widespread popularity after its invention in the late 1800s. British soldiers stationed in tropical countries began to add gin and lime juice to their anti-malaria tonic. The gin and citrus mellowed the bitterness of the quinine, making a surprisingly delicious cocktail that has remained popular ever since.

INSTRUCTIONS:

Fill a tall glass with ice. Add the gin and lime juice and stir to chill. Top with the tonic water and garnish with a lime wedge.

THE ORIGINS OF GIN

Although spirits made with juniper berries have been around since at least the 11th century, the gin we know and love today originated in England in the mid-1600s. When the malty, juniper-flavored spirit jenever arrived in England from the Netherlands, it became tremendously popular. As the demand grew, distilleries in England began producing a jenever variation that would soon become gin.

By the early 1700s, gin production in England was booming, due in part to a series of Acts of Parliament that would make it easy for new distilleries to open and for anyone to legally distill spirits at home. Unfortunately, much of this homemade gin was of very poor quality and was often made with harmful chemicals. Gin began to develop an unsavory reputation, and its widespread overconsumption led to an array of health and social issues. Parliament subsequently passed the Gin Act to try to control the "gin craze." By the early 1800s, gin production was becoming more refined, and several brands emerged with much higher-quality products.

As the quality of gin increased, so too did its worldwide popularity. The ban on the export of gin was lifted in 1850, and the spirit began to star in a variety of now-classic American cocktails. Gin's popularity remained high throughout Prohibition, and its association with cocktail culture and the upper class was solidified by the 1930s. Interest declined for several decades until it was revived in the 1980s with the introduction of several new craft gins. Today, there are more producers of gin than ever, and there is an endless selection of brands and styles. With both classic and modern gin-based cocktails dominating cocktail menus around the world, gin's popularity shows no sign of letting up any time soon.

NEGRONI

1 ounce gin

1 ounce Campari

1 ounce sweet vermouth

Orange twist, for garnish

The infamous bittersweet cocktail takes its name from its alleged inventor, Italian Count Negroni. The legend says that the Count asked for a stronger version of the popular Americano cocktail, prompting the bartender to replace the soda water with gin. Although historians debate whether the Count actually existed, the story and the cocktail have lived on.

INSTRUCTIONS:

Combine the gin, Campari, and vermouth in a mixing glass. Fill ¾ of the glass with ice. Stir until chilled, about 30 seconds. Strain the drink into a rocks glass filled with ice (or one large cube). Garnish with an expressed orange twist.

ESSENTIAL 3-INGREDIENT COCKTAILS

BEE'S KNEES

2 ounces gin

¾ ounce lemon juice

¾ ounce
honey syrup
(see page 31)

Lemon twist,
for garnish

"The bee's knees" was Prohibition-era slang for something fantastic, and this cocktail is just that. Originally created to make the harsh, bathtub gins of the time more palatable, this classic recipe is still a great way to enjoy gin. Floral honey pairs beautifully with gin's botanical flavors, while the lemon juice brightens and balances.

INSTRUCTIONS:

Combine the gin, lemon juice, and syrup in a cocktail shaker. Fill ¾ of the shaker with ice. Shake until chilled, about 12 seconds. Strain the drink into a coupe glass and garnish with an expressed lemon twist.

GIN RICKEY

1½ ounces gin

½ ounce lime juice

6 ounces
sparkling water

Lime wheel,
for garnish

The gin rickey is the ultimate cool-off cocktail for hot summer days. The rickey was named for its inventor, a political figure in Washington, DC, named Joe Rickey. Though it was originally made with whiskey, gin soon became the favored spirit, and many other variations followed. Crisp and unsweetened, the gin rickey is one of the lightest and easiest cocktails you can make at home.

INSTRUCTIONS:

Fill a tall glass with ice. Add the gin and lime juice and stir to chill. Top with the chilled sparkling water and garnish with a lime wheel.

COSMONAUT

2 ounces gin

¾ ounce lemon juice

1 barspoon
raspberry jam

The cosmonaut is one of several modern classic cocktails to originate at Sasha Petraske's New York City bar Milk & Honey. Sasha himself is credited with the cosmonaut recipe, which pokes fun at the popular (yet not always very balanced) cocktail the cosmopolitan. Fresh, fruity, and made with readily available ingredients, the cosmonaut is easy to enjoy any time of year.

INSTRUCTIONS:
Combine the gin, lemon juice, and jam in a cocktail shaker. Fill ¾ of the shaker with ice. Shake until chilled, about 12 seconds. Fine strain the drink into a coupe glass.

ALASKA

1½ ounces gin

½ ounce yellow Chartreuse

1 dash orange bitters

Lemon twist, for garnish

The classic Alaska cocktail is a martini variation that replaces dry vermouth with the potent, herbal liqueur Chartreuse. The Alaska calls for yellow Chartreuse, which is a bit more mild than the green variety, but it still packs a flavorful punch. The first mention of the Alaska cocktail appeared in Harry Craddock's The Savoy Cocktail Book *in 1930, although it's unclear how it came to acquire its name.*

INSTRUCTIONS:

Combine the gin, Chartreuse, and bitters in a mixing glass. Fill ¾ of the glass with ice. Stir until chilled, about 30 seconds. Strain the drink into a martini glass and garnish with an expressed lemon twist.

ESSENTIAL 3-INGREDIENT COCKTAILS

BABY BRAMBLE

2 ounces gin

1 ounce lemon juice

1 ounce blackberry
syrup (see page 34)

Lemon wheel,
for garnish

Blackberry,
for garnish

The baby bramble is my ultra-simplified version of the modern classic gin cocktail the bramble. First introduced by Dick Bradsell in the 1980s, the bramble is a refreshing mix of gin, lemon juice, and simple syrup, topped with crème de mure (blackberry liqueur). Crème de mure can be a tough ingredient to find, so this easy version replaces the syrup and liqueur with homemade blackberry syrup for loads of fresh berry flavor.

INSTRUCTIONS:

Combine the gin, lemon juice, and syrup in a cocktail shaker. Fill ¾ of the shaker with ice. Shake until chilled, about 12 seconds. Strain the drink into a rocks glass filled with ice and garnish with a lemon wheel and a blackberry.

ELDERFLOWER GIMLET

1½ ounces gin

¾ ounce
elderflower liqueur

¾ ounce lime juice

Lime wheel,
for garnish

Elderflower liqueur is an immensely popular ingredient among professional bartenders and home bartenders alike. It adds a rich, beautifully floral and somewhat fruity flavor to cocktails. It complements many spirits but pairs especially well with the botanicals in gin. The gimlet is a classic gin cocktail made with lime juice and simple syrup. For this recipe, I've replaced the simple syrup with elderflower liqueur for a simple, yet flavorful upgrade.

INSTRUCTIONS:

Combine the gin, elderflower liqueur, and lime juice in a cocktail shaker. Fill ¾ of the shaker with ice. Shake until chilled, about 12 seconds. Strain the drink into a coupe glass and garnish with a lime wheel.

ESSENTIAL 3-INGREDIENT COCKTAILS

ROSEMARY GREYHOUND

1½ ounces gin

½ ounce rosemary
syrup (see page 33)

4 ounces pink
grapefruit juice

Rosemary sprig,
for garnish

The greyhound is one of the very simplest cocktails: spirit plus grapefruit juice. Though it's typically made with either gin or vodka, I enjoy mine with the kick of juniper from gin and an upgrade of herbal flavor. I've added a touch of rosemary syrup for complexity and used freshly squeezed pink grapefruit juice for a very refreshing, very pretty, winter seasonal sipper.

INSTRUCTIONS:

Fill a rocks glass with ice. Add the gin, syrup, and grapefruit juice and stir gently. Garnish with a sprig of fresh rosemary.

PINK GIN PALOMA

2 ounces pink gin

½ ounce lime juice

6 ounces
grapefruit soda

Grapefruit slice,
for garnish

Pink gins are a popular new wave of fruit-forward spirits that are flavored with pink or red botanicals such as grapefruits, strawberries, raspberries, or red currants. I really enjoy the Gin Rosa from Malfy Gin, which has a wonderful, natural pink grapefruit flavor. Other popular options include the berry-flavored Gordon's Pink Gin and Beefeater Pink. This pink gin paloma is a crisp and fruity variation of the classic paloma, which is traditionally made with tequila or mezcal.

INSTRUCTIONS:
Fill a highball glass with ice. Add the gin and lime juice and stir to chill. Top with the grapefruit soda and garnish with a slice of grapefruit.

PINK GIN PALOMA, PAGE 70

ESPRESSO MARTINI, PAGE 76

VODKA

MOSCOW MULE

2 ounces vodka

½ ounce lime juice

6 ounces
ginger beer

Lime wheel,
for garnish

The Moscow mule was first served up in the early 1940s in Los Angeles. John G. Martin, the new owner of Smirnoff Vodka in the United States, and Jack Morgan, a bar owner, are the most frequently attributed inventors of the drink. The story goes: Martin was looking to find a way to get Americans to drink more vodka, and Morgan had a surplus of ginger beer on his hands. For the best Moscow mule, use a flavorful and spicy ginger beer, such as Fever-Tree's ginger beer.

INSTRUCTIONS:

Fill a mule mug or a highball glass with ice. Add the vodka and lime juice and stir to chill. Top with the ginger beer and garnish with a lime wheel.

ESSENTIAL 3-INGREDIENT COCKTAILS

WHITE RUSSIAN

2 ounces vodka

1 ounce
coffee liqueur

1 ounce cream

The White Russian is one of the most indulgent and visually appealing dessert cocktails, combining a dark layer of vodka and coffee liqueur with a hit of cream. Although it was first invented as far back as the late 1940s, it wasn't a very popular cocktail until the 1998 movie The Big Lebowski *showcased it as the main character's drink of choice.*

INSTRUCTIONS:

Fill a rocks glass with ice. Add the vodka and coffee liqueur and stir until chilled. Top with the cold cream. Stir gently before serving.

ESPRESSO MARTINI

1½ ounces vodka

1 ounce freshly
brewed espresso

1 ounce
coffee liqueur

Coffee beans,
for garnish

The espresso martini, while not technically a martini, is a sweet, strong, coffee-based cocktail. With freshly brewed espresso, this caffein-ated cocktail is a great way to begin a night out (or keep the night going). The espresso martini is another modern classic cocktail attributed to London bartender Dick Bradsell during vodka's heyday in the 1980s.

INSTRUCTIONS:

Combine the vodka, espresso, and coffee liqueur in a cocktail shaker. Fill ¾ of the shaker with ice. Shake until chilled, about 12 seconds. Strain the drink into a martini glass and garnish with coffee beans.

ESSENTIAL 3-INGREDIENT COCKTAILS

GIMLET

2 ounces vodka

¾ ounce lime juice

¾ ounce simple
syrup (see page 30)

Lime wheel,
for garnish

Gimlets are simple sour-style cocktails made with either vodka or gin, lime juice, and simple syrup. Traditionally, the gimlet was made with equal parts spirit and Rose's lime cordial, a bottled sweetened lime juice. This modern gimlet recipe opts for freshly squeezed lime juice and simple syrup instead, which strikes a triple balance among sweet, sour, and the strength of the vodka.

INSTRUCTIONS:

Combine the vodka, lime juice, and syrup in a cocktail shaker. Fill ¾ of the shaker with ice. Shake until chilled, about 12 seconds. Strain the drink into a coupe glass and garnish with a lime wheel.

THE ORIGINS OF VODKA

Vodka's history begins in either Russia or Poland, depending on who you ask. Vodka may have been distilled in Russia as early as the 12th century, and it was well established there by the 1500s. The history of vodka in Poland appears to have begun in the 1400s. Interestingly, we might know more about vodka's history if it weren't for an unfortunate turn of events in the 1600s. The Russian Orthodox Church declared vodka an "invention of the devil" and sought to destroy all documentation about the spirit's history and production.

Originally intended as medicine, vodka evolved into a popular drink in 16th-century Russia, enjoyed at weddings and other celebratory occasions. Increased popularity led to increased public drunkenness, eventually inciting laws that restricted alcohol consumption to only certain days. By the late 1700s, Polish vodka was being made from potatoes, marking an improvement in quality and smoothness. In the 1860s, the biggest improvement to vodka quality was made when the spirit was filtered through charcoal. For the first time, vodka was colorless and neutral-tasting. Vodka sales and consumption continued to be tightly regulated, leading to an increase in home distilling. The Bolshevik Revolution in the early 1900s banned the production of vodka and led many family producers to leave the country, allowing vodka to spread abroad.

Vodka made its way to America and France in the 1920s, leading to the invention of the classic Bloody Mary in Paris, most likely by bartender Fernand Petiot. Vodka took a while to get established in America, but by the 1940s, drinkers began to prefer clear spirits to brown ones for their ability to mix well with a variety of juices. Like gin, vodka's popularity declined until the 1980s, when exciting new cocktails like the cosmopolitan helped launch the spirit into the spotlight again.

VESPER

1 ounce vodka

3 ounces gin

½ ounce Lillet Blanc

Lemon twist,
for garnish

The vesper is a unique cocktail because it was invented not by a bartender, but by an author. In Ian Fleming's famous 1953 book, Casino Royale, *James Bond first orders this potent martini variation. This bold cocktail is bone-dry and not for the faint of heart—it contains as much alcohol as two standard cocktails!*

INSTRUCTIONS:

Combine the vodka, gin, and Lillet Blanc in a mixing glass. Fill ¾ of the glass with ice. Stir until chilled, about 30 seconds. Strain the drink into a martini glass and garnish with an expressed lemon twist.

ESSENTIAL 3-INGREDIENT COCKTAILS

KAMIKAZE

2 ounces vodka

1 ounce triple sec

1 ounce lime juice

Lime wedge, for garnish

The kamikaze is perhaps best known as a "shooter," being first served up in shot glass–sized portions in bars during the 1970s and 1980s. In its long form, the cocktail is essentially a vodka margarita, balancing orange liqueur and lime juice with vodka instead of tequila.

INSTRUCTIONS:

Combine the vodka, triple sec, and lime juice in a cocktail shaker. Fill ¾ of the shaker with ice. Shake until chilled, about 12 seconds. Strain the drink into a coupe glass and garnish with a lime wedge.

SALTY DOG

Coarse salt

2 ounces vodka

4 ounces
grapefruit juice

Grapefruit slice,
for garnish

The salty dog is a salted variation of the classic greyhound cocktail, combining vodka or gin with grapefruit juice. Salt enhances both the sweet and sour flavors of the grapefruit juice, making it a very crisp and satisfying drink on a hot summer afternoon.

INSTRUCTIONS:

Rim a highball glass with coarse salt and fill with ice. Add the vodka and grapefruit juice and stir gently. Garnish with a grapefruit slice.

ESSENTIAL 3-INGREDIENT COCKTAILS

SEA BREEZE

The sea breeze is a favorite summer cooler, featuring the sweet-tart flavors of cranberry and grapefruit. This cocktail is easy to batch for a group and is always a crowd-pleaser. Simply multiply the recipe below by the number of guests, add all the ingredients to a large pitcher, and stir.

1½ ounces vodka

3 ounces
cranberry juice

1½ ounces
grapefruit juice

Lime wedge,
for garnish

INSTRUCTIONS:

Fill a highball glass with ice. Add the vodka, cranberry juice, and grapefruit juice and stir gently. Garnish with a lime wedge.

LEMON DROP

2 ounces vodka

1 ounce triple sec

1 ounce lemon juice

Sugar, for garnish

Like many popular vodka cocktails, the lemon drop first appeared in the 1970s. Invented by Norman Jay Hobday in his San Francisco bar, Henry Africa's, the cocktail was a hit. It waned in popularity in the 1990s, but when Oprah Winfrey famously made lemon drops on her television show in 2006, she put the sweet and citrusy cocktail back on the map.

INSTRUCTIONS:

Rim a martini glass with sugar (optional). Combine the vodka, triple sec, and lemon juice in a cocktail shaker. Fill ¾ of the shaker with ice. Shake until chilled, about 12 seconds. Strain the drink into the sugared martini glass.

ESSENTIAL 3-INGREDIENT COCKTAILS

SPA DAY

2 ounces vodka

¾ ounce lemon juice

¾ ounce mint syrup
(see page 32)

Mint leaf,
for garnish

The spa day is a simple vodka sour I created with fresh lemon and cool mint. This easygoing cocktail is light and uplifting any time, but it's especially good on a day off or following a massage or a dip in a hot tub. On weekends, I often mix up cocktails on the fly with whatever ingredients I have on hand. The spa day is one of those improvised recipes that I've enjoyed making again and again.

INSTRUCTIONS:
Combine the vodka, lemon juice, and syrup in a cocktail shaker. Fill ¾ of the shaker with ice. Shake until chilled, about 12 seconds. Strain the drink into a coupe glass and garnish with a mint leaf.

BLOODY MARY

2 ounces vodka

½ ounce lemon juice

6 ounces Bloody
Mary mix

Celery stalk,
for garnish

Invented in Paris in the 1920s as a mix of vodka and tomato juice, the Bloody Mary was perhaps the first widely popular vodka cocktail. In the 1930s, the cocktail made its way to America where spices and citrus were added, creating the cocktail we know today. Although you can certainly create your own Bloody Mary mix at home if you prefer, there are several excellent mixes on the market that make creating this cocktail a breeze. I enjoy the mixes from Bloody Gerry and Cocktail Artist.

INSTRUCTIONS:

Fill a highball glass with ice. Add the vodka, lemon juice, and Bloody Mary mix and stir to chill. Garnish with a celery stalk.

ESSENTIAL 3-INGREDIENT COCKTAILS

BLOODY MARY, PAGE 86

HONEYSUCKLE DAIQUIRI, PAGE 99

RUM

CUBA LIBRE

2 ounces white rum

½ ounce lime juice

4 ounces cola

Lime wheel,
for garnish

While it's unclear exactly how or when the Cuba Libre *(meaning "Free Cuba") was invented most agree it was first created sometime around 1900, when Coca-Cola was first imported to Cuba. A perpetual crowd-pleaser, the easygoing mix of rum, citrus, and cola is one of the most popular mixed drinks in the world.*

TIP: **Some say a Cuba libre tastes best when mixed with Mexican Coca-Cola, which is made with sugar instead of corn syrup and packaged in glass bottles rather than cans.**

INSTRUCTIONS:
Fill a highball glass with ice. Add the rum and lime juice and stir gently. Top with the cola and garnish with a lime wheel.

ESSENTIAL 3-INGREDIENT COCKTAILS

DARK SKIES

1½ ounces dark rum

½ ounce lime juice

4 ounces
ginger beer

Lime wedge,
for garnish

This drink is fashioned after the famous Dark 'n Stormy trademarked by Gosling's Rum. The classic was invented in Bermuda after World War I when British naval officers realized that spicy ginger beer was the perfect complement to full-bodied Gosling's Rum. While the Dark 'n Stormy is made with Gosling's Black Seal rum, Gosling's ginger beer, and an optional lime wedge, this variation adds ½ ounce of lime juice to cut the sweetness of the drink. Quality ingredients are important, but this version can be made with any dark rum and ginger beer you like.

INSTRUCTIONS:

Fill a highball glass with ice. Add the rum and lime juice and stir gently. Top with the ginger beer and garnish with a lime wedge.

RUM

DAIQUIRI

2 ounces white rum

1 ounce lime juice

¾ ounce simple syrup (see page 30)

Not to be confused with the overly sweetened, made-from-a-mix, frozen daiquiris you'll find at chain restaurants, the classic daiquiri is served up simply and perfectly balanced. The daiquiri is said to have been invented in Cuba in 1898 by an American mining engineer named Jennings Cox. He reportedly created the drink after running out of gin at a party and named it for Daiquiri, the village he was living in at the time.

INSTRUCTIONS:

Put the rum, lime juice, and syrup in a cocktail shaker. Fill ¾ of the shaker with ice. Shake until chilled, about 12 seconds. Strain the drink into a coupe glass.

ESSENTIAL 3-INGREDIENT COCKTAILS

GROG

2 ounces dark rum

¾ ounce lime juice

¾ ounce demerara syrup (see page 31)

Lime wedge, for garnish

Today, the word grog brings to mind images of swashbuckling, rum-guzzling pirates, but this old-school cocktail was actually invented by the British Navy. Water was added to the rum to slow the effects of the alcohol and prevent over-intoxication. They also sometimes added lime juice and sugar to make the drink more palatable, birthing a tasty rum cocktail. Grog is a refreshing, richly flavored aged-rum cocktail that can be a great introduction to the world of tiki-style cocktails.

INSTRUCTIONS:

Put the rum, lime juice, syrup, and 2 ounces of water in a cocktail shaker. Fill ¾ of the shaker with ice. Shake until chilled, about 12 seconds. Strain the drink into a rocks glass and garnish with a lime wedge.

THE ORIGINS OF RUM

Rum, as we know it today, originated in the West Indies in the 1600s. It's believed that the first of these rums was made in Barbados from accidentally fermented molasses. Rum's popularity spread throughout the Caribbean and to Colonial North America by the mid-1600s. Colonial New England became an important center of rum production in America, where it was the most popular spirit until whiskey surpassed it in the 1800s. At the height of its popularity, the average colonist drank about seven shots of the stuff per day! Even George Washington was fond of it, having imported barrels of fine Barbados rum served at his inauguration as the first president of the United States.

Rum's famed popularity with the British Royal Navy began shortly after the capture of Jamaica in 1655. Each sailor's daily ration of imported brandy was replaced with rum, a tradition that continued until 1970.

Initially, all rums were generally unaged. Aged rum was invented accidentally when rum barrels awaiting shipment sat for long periods. Drinkers noticed an improved, smoother flavor, and eventually rum makers would produce and categorize rums by their age and subsequent color. Dark rums are typically those aged at least five years; gold rums are aged for about three years; and light, or white, rums are usually aged for just one year.

TI' PUNCH

1½ ounces white
rhum agricole

¼ ounce demerara
syrup (see page 31)

1 lime slice

Ti' Punch, *meaning "little punch," is the national cocktail of the Caribbean island of Martinique. Martinique is known for its rhum agricole, which is a flavorful style of rum made from freshly squeezed sugarcane juice. This very small rhum cocktail is unique in its no-fuss, ice-optional preparation. The Ti' Punch is traditionally served as a glass of rhum agricole with lime and sweetener on the side so that patrons can adjust it to their own taste. This version is an excellent introduction to the world of rhum agricole and a fun and easygoing alternative to the daiquiri.*

INSTRUCTIONS:

Put the rhum agricole and syrup in a rocks glass. Squeeze the lime slice into the glass, and drop it in. Using a swizzle stick or spoon, stir all the ingredients. Add ice, if desired.

ESSENTIAL 3-INGREDIENT COCKTAILS

RUM FLIP

2 ounces dark rum

½ ounce demerara syrup (see page 31)

1 whole egg

Freshly grated nutmeg, for garnish

Flip-style drinks have been around for as long as folks have been making cocktails. Originally made with both spirit (often rum) and beer and served hot, the flip eventually evolved into a chilled cocktail made with rum, sweetener, and a whole egg. The addition of eggs to cocktails rounds out harsh flavors and produces a rich froth with a velvety mouthfeel. The rum flip was mentioned in the 1862 bar book How to Mix Drinks *by legendary bartender Jerry Thomas.*

INSTRUCTIONS:

Put the rum, syrup, and egg in a cocktail shaker. Shake vigorously for about 30 seconds to froth the egg. Open the shaker and fill ¾ of it with ice. Shake for an additional 12 seconds or so until chilled. Strain the drink into a coupe glass and garnish with nutmeg.

RUM OLD-FASHIONED

2 ounces dark rum

¼ ounce demerara syrup (see page 31)

2 dashes Angostura bitters

Orange twist, for garnish

The rum old-fashioned takes a classic old-fashioned and replaces the whiskey with aged rum. High-quality aged rums are excellent sipped neat or served in spirit-forward cocktails, allowing the drinker to experience the full range of flavors. The reason that rum old-fashioneds are such a great introduction to spirit-forward cocktails is that aged rums have a smoothness and sweetness that many whiskeys do not.

INSTRUCTIONS:

Combine the rum, syrup, and bitters in a mixing glass. Fill ¾ of the glass with ice. Stir until chilled, about 30 seconds. Strain the drink into a rocks glass filled with ice and garnish with an expressed orange twist.

HONEYSUCKLE DAIQUIRI

2 ounces white rum

¾ ounce honey
syrup (see page 31)

¾ ounce lime juice

Lime slice,
for garnish

Edible flower, for
garnish (optional)

The honeysuckle daiquiri first appeared in David Embury's 1948 cocktail book The Fine Art of Mixing Drinks. *This daiquiri riff has had many variations over the years, using both lemon and lime juices and adding some orange juice, but I think this cocktail really shines with the simple, sharp contrast of the sour lime with the floral sweetness of honey.*

INSTRUCTIONS:

Put the rum, syrup, and lime juice in a cocktail shaker. Fill ¾ of the shaker with ice. Shake until chilled, about 12 seconds. Strain the drink into a coupe glass and garnish with a lime slice and an edible flower (if using).

ARCHIPELAGO

2 ounces dark rum

1 ounce lime juice

½ ounce orgeat

Sprig of mint, for garnish

This tiki-style rum sour is my simplified version of the classic mai tai, which is made with aged rums, lime juice, orange liqueur, and orgeat. The archipelago omits the orange liqueur in favor of a larger dose of almond-flavored orgeat syrup to enhance the deep, toasted flavors of the aged rum. A garnish of fresh mint adds a cooling, fresh aroma that makes this cocktail ideal for lazy afternoons at the beach.

INSTRUCTIONS:

Put the rum, lime juice, and orgeat in a cocktail shaker. Fill ¾ of the shaker with ice. Shake until chilled, about 12 seconds. Strain the drink into a rocks glass filled with ice and garnish with a sprig of mint.

ESSENTIAL 3-INGREDIENT COCKTAILS

SUNRISE MARGARITA, PAGE 113

TEQUILA & MEZCAL

MARGARITA

2 ounces tequila
or mezcal

1 ounce lime juice

1 ounce triple sec

Lime wedge,
for garnish

Since its invention, the margarita has been served up, on the rocks, and frozen and made with a variety of nontraditional ingredients, including bottled mixes. I highly recommend avoiding bottled margarita mixes—bottled sour mixes can't compare with the flavor of fresh citrus juices.

TIP: **There is no hard and fast rule for how to serve a margarita, so feel free to experiment with serving it up, in a coupe glass, or blending it with a scoop of crushed ice for a refreshing frozen cocktail.**

INSTRUCTIONS:

Put the tequila, lime juice, and triple sec in a cocktail shaker. Fill ¾ of the shaker with ice. Shake until chilled, about 12 seconds. Strain the drink into a rocks glass filled with ice and garnish with a lime wedge.

ESSENTIAL 3-INGREDIENT COCKTAILS

TOMMY'S MARGARITA

2 ounces
100 percent blue
agave tequila

1 ounce lime juice

½ ounce agave syrup

Lime wedge,
for garnish

Tommy's Margarita is a popular variation on the classic that substitutes orange liqueur for agave syrup. It was invented in the 1990s by Julio Bermejo at Tommy's Mexican Restaurant in San Francisco, California. Bermejo's margarita variation was unique at the time for its use of agave syrup and 100 percent blue agave tequila. Tequilas made with less than 51 percent blue agave, or tequila "mixto," were less expensive and more commonly used in cocktails at the time.

INSTRUCTIONS:

Put the tequila, lime juice, and syrup in a cocktail shaker. Fill ¾ of the shaker with ice. Shake until chilled, about 12 seconds. Strain the drink into a rocks glass filled with ice and garnish with a lime wedge.

PALOMA

2 ounces tequila
or mezcal

Juice of ½ lime

6 ounces
grapefruit soda

Lime slice,
for garnish

Although the margarita is the most popular tequila cocktail in the United States, it's often said that the paloma is Mexico's favorite cocktail. The sweet-and-sour mix of grapefruit soda, lime, and tequila or mezcal is even easier to make than a margarita, requiring minimal measuring and no shaking. The invention of the paloma is often credited to Don Javier Delgado Corona, owner of La Capilla, a bar in Tequila, Mexico. The paloma can be made with any tequila or mezcal, but the smoky, earthy flavors of mezcal pair beautifully with crisp, slightly floral grapefruit.

INSTRUCTIONS:

Fill a highball glass with ice. Add the tequila and lime juice and stir gently to chill. Top with the chilled grapefruit soda and garnish with a lime slice.

ESSENTIAL 3-INGREDIENT COCKTAILS

AGAVE OLD-FASHIONED

2 ounces aged
tequila or mezcal

¼ ounce agave syrup

2 dashes
Angostura bitters

Orange twist,
for garnish

The old-fashioned is an excellent format for enjoying the full range of flavors of premium or aged spirits, tequila and mezcal included. Depending on your personal preference, you can make an old-fashioned with tequila, mezcal, or even a combination of the two spirits. New York City bartender Phil Ward is often noted as helping to proliferate the use of tequila, especially mezcal, in craft cocktails. Ward invented the famous Oaxacan Old-Fashioned in 2007, a blend of three parts tequila, one part mezcal, agave syrup, and bitters.

INSTRUCTIONS:

Combine the tequila, syrup, and bitters in a mixing glass. Fill ¾ of the glass with ice. Stir until chilled, about 30 seconds. Strain the drink into a rocks glass filled with ice and garnish with an expressed orange twist.

TEQUILA & MEZCAL

THE ORIGINS OF TEQUILA AND MEZCAL

Although several alcoholic agave-based beverages originated in Mexico, the earliest was a drink made with fermented agave sap, known as pulque. This was the primary agave-based drink in Mexico until distillation arrived with the Spanish conquistadors in the 1500s. The first distilled agave spirit, mezcal, was created in 1530. Mezcal, literally meaning "oven-cooked agave," can be made with any variety of agave plant. Tequila is a type of mezcal made only with the blue agave, and it must be produced within certain regions in Mexico. Modern-day tequila's roots date back to 1600, though it didn't acquire its official definition until the early 1900s.

Early mezcals produced in the town of Tequila were recognized for their high quality and spread quickly throughout the country because of Tequila's ideal location on an established shipping route. Mezcal production was driven underground for a period in the late 1780s until 1795, when a new Spanish king, Ferdinand IV, lifted the previous king's ban. That year, Don Jose Maria Guadalupe de Cuervo was given the first official license to produce mezcal, and the first legal distillery was established in the town of Tequila.

In 1873, Sauza tequila was the first to be exported to the United States. Other brands followed, and "mezcal brandy," as it was known in the States at the time, gradually grew in popularity. The invention of the margarita cocktail sometime in the 1930s or 1940s increased that popularity exponentially, making it one of the most popular spirits in the world. Today, agave spirits can be found in bars all over the world. Tequila and mezcal are now common ingredients in craft cocktails, ranging from Old-Fashioneds (page 42) to Bloody Marias (page 112).

MATADOR

1½ ounces tequila

½ ounce lime juice

2 ounces
unsweetened
pineapple juice

Pineapple
wedge,
for garnish

A cousin of the margarita, the matador uses a healthy pour of unsweetened pineapple juice to add sweetness, rather than a liqueur or syrup. Tasty, simple, and easy to make, the matador is a crowd-pleasing cocktail that batches easily for a group.

INSTRUCTIONS:

Put the tequila, lime juice, and pineapple juice in a cocktail shaker. Fill ¾ of the shaker with ice. Shake briefly, just until combined (to prevent overdilution). Strain the drink into a rocks glass filled with ice and garnish with a wedge of pineapple.

TIP: If hosting a party, multiply the ingredients by the number of your guests, add all the ingredients to a pitcher, and stir to combine. Chill in the refrigerator until it's time to serve.

ESSENTIAL 3-INGREDIENT COCKTAILS

EL REY

2 ounces tequila

½ ounce triple sec

1 ounce dry vermouth

Lemon twist, for garnish

El rey (meaning "the king" in Spanish) is a tequila-based riff on the classic rum cocktail El Presidente, which combines white rum with dry vermouth, orange liqueur, and a bit of grenadine. While experimenting with tequila martini variations, I created this cocktail on a whim and loved it. I later recognized its similarity to the classic rum cocktail and gave this riff a proper name.

INSTRUCTIONS:

Combine the tequila, triple sec, and vermouth in a mixing glass. Fill ¾ of the glass with ice. Stir until chilled, about 30 seconds. Strain the drink into a coupe glass and garnish with an expressed lemon twist.

BLOODY MARIA

2 ounces
tequila blanco

½ ounce lime juice

6 ounces Bloody
Mary mix

Lime wedge,
for garnish

This Bloody Mary variation is perhaps even better than the original vodka-based cocktail, combining earthy tequila with vegetal tomato juice. Like the classic Bloody Mary, you can opt to use your own homemade mix, or choose from the many bottled Bloody Mary mixes on the market. Simply mix tequila with a squeeze of lime and your preferred Bloody Mary mix. If you like it spicy, you can garnish with a dash or two of hot sauce, or even pickled jalapeño slices.

INSTRUCTIONS:

Fill a highball glass with ice. Add the tequila, lime juice, and Bloody Mary mix and stir to chill. Garnish with a lime wedge.

ESSENTIAL 3-INGREDIENT COCKTAILS

SUNRISE MARGARITA

2 ounces tequila

1 ounce lime juice

½ ounce grenadine

Lime wedge,
for garnish

This margarita variation was inspired by the tequila sunrise, a layered cocktail made with tequila, orange juice, and grenadine. It is quite sweet and benefits from the addition of lemon or lime juice. Interestingly, early recipes for the tequila sunrise called for a very different mix that included lime juice and blackcurrant liqueur (crème de cassis). Inspired by those recipes, I created the sunrise margarita to balance sweet and sour while maintaining the signature red hue from pomegranate-based grenadine syrup.

INSTRUCTIONS:

Put the tequila, lime juice, and grenadine in a cocktail shaker. Fill ¾ of the shaker with ice. Shake until chilled, about 12 seconds. Strain the drink into a rocks glass filled with ice and garnish with a lime wedge.

TEQUILA & MEZCAL

MIDNIGHT IN OAXACA

1½ ounces mezcal

¾ ounce Amaro
Montenegro

¾ ounce
coffee liqueur

Orange twist,
for garnish

Smoky and earthy mezcal, complex Italian amaro, and the richness of coffee liqueur come together to form a dark and delicious nightcap in the midnight in Oaxaca. I created this cocktail as an ode to my love of each of these three ingredients. Mezcal is the star of the show, so choose a bottle with plenty of character. Coffee liqueur adds a sweet, chocolate-like flavor that balances the strong herbal flavors of the amaro. An expressed orange twist uplifts this blend of heavy flavors, so don't skip the garnish.

INSTRUCTIONS:

Combine the mezcal and liqueurs in a mixing glass. Fill ¾ of the glass with ice. Stir until chilled, about 30 seconds. Strain the drink into a rocks glass filled with ice and garnish with an expressed orange twist.

PARAISO

2 ounces tequila

¾ ounce lime juice

¾ ounce
hibiscus syrup
(see page 33)

Lime wheel,
for garnish

Tequila, hibiscus, and lime are a tropical cocktail dream team. Simple, fruity, and refreshing, the paraiso (meaning "paradise" in Spanish) is an excellent choice when you're looking for something laid-back, summery, and even Instagrammable. I created the paraiso as a fun warm-weather party cocktail with easy-to-remember measurements and a beautiful red hue. Give this cocktail even more tropical flair by garnishing with an edible flower, such as an orchid.

INSTRUCTIONS:

Put the tequila, lime juice, and syrup in a cocktail shaker. Fill ¾ of the shaker with ice. Shake until chilled, about 12 seconds. Strain the drink into a coupe glass and garnish with a lime wheel.

SOLAR FLARE

2 ounces mezcal

1 ounce lemon juice

¾ ounce passion
fruit syrup

Lemon slice,
for garnish

The solar flare is a tropical mix of smoky mezcal, lemon, and passion fruit. I created this fruity, sweet, and sour recipe as an introductory mezcal cocktail for those new to the spirit. I enjoy making the solar flare with Liber & Co's passion fruit syrup. These days, passion fruit syrup is relatively easy to find in grocery stores or liquor stores, but you could also substitute a passion fruit liqueur, or make your own passion fruit syrup using equal parts ripe fruit, sugar, and water.

INSTRUCTIONS:

Put the mezcal, lemon juice, and syrup in a cocktail shaker. Fill ¾ of the shaker with ice. Shake until chilled, about 12 seconds. Strain the cocktail into a rocks glass filled with ice and garnish with a lemon slice.

DOCTOR'S ORDERS

2 ounces mezcal

¾ ounce ginger
honey syrup
(see page 31)

¾ ounce lemon juice

Candied ginger,
for garnish

Doctor's orders was inspired by a modern classic cocktail, the penicillin. Invented in New York City around 2000 by bartender Sam Ross, the penicillin contains blended Scotch whiskey, lemon, honey, ginger, and a hint of Islay single malt whiskey. The smoky, spicy, and sweet cocktail is like an adult cold remedy, although much more delicious. Using the primary flavors of Ross's original, I created a simple agave variation that lets the smokiness of mezcal shine.

INSTRUCTIONS:

Put the mezcal, syrup, and lemon juice in a cocktail shaker. Fill ¾ of the shaker with ice. Shake until chilled, about 12 seconds. Strain the drink into a coupe glass and garnish with candied ginger on a cocktail pick.

GRASSHOPPER, PAGE 130

CHAPTER 8

BONUS COCKTAILS

BRANDY ALEXANDER

1½ ounces Cognac

1 ounce crème
de cacao

1 ounce cream

Freshly grated
nutmeg,
for garnish

The brandy Alexander is the best-known Alexander cocktail today, but interestingly, the original Alexander was made with gin. The brandy Alexander is an indulgent blend of Cognac, crème de cacao, and cream, making it a fantastic dessert drink. Although not as common as many other 3-ingredient cocktails, the brandy Alexander has had a few moments in the spotlight, including being noted as a favorite drink of musician John Lennon.

INSTRUCTIONS:

Put the Cognac, crème de cacao, and cream in a cocktail shaker. Fill ¾ of the shaker with ice. Shake until chilled, about 12 seconds. Strain the drink into a martini glass and garnish with nutmeg.

SIDECAR

2 ounces Cognac

1 ounce triple sec

¾ ounce lemon juice

Lemon twist,
for garnish

It's unknown who created or named the drink, but there are stories placing the cocktail in both Paris and London in the 1920s. Beyond the cocktail's origins, one of the hottest debates regarding the sidecar is the correct proportion of each ingredient to use. Some recipes use less orange liqueur, some use more, and others use a sugared rim to add sweetness to drier interpretations of the drink. My preferred recipe has a strong Cognac punch, rounded by a balance of sweet and sour flavors.

INSTRUCTIONS:

Put the Cognac, triple sec, and lemon juice in a cocktail shaker. Fill ¾ of the shaker with ice. Shake until chilled, about 12 seconds. Strain the drink into a coupe glass and garnish with an expressed lemon twist.

COGNAC OLD-FASHIONED

2 ounces Cognac

¼ ounce simple
syrup (see page 30)

2 dashes
Angostura bitters

Orange twist,
for garnish

If you enjoy sipping Cognac neat, the Cognac old-fashioned is a wonderful alternative way to experience the spirit. With its smooth character and depth of flavor, Cognac is an ideal spirit for the simple format of the old-fashioned. Cognac's flavors run the gamut from toasted breads to vanilla, cinnamon, fruit, and even chocolate. A touch of sweetness, some bitters, and just enough dilution open up the spirit, making more flavors readily accessible to the drinker.

INSTRUCTIONS:

Combine the Cognac, syrup, and bitters in a mixing glass. Fill ¾ of the glass with ice. Stir until chilled, about 30 seconds. Strain the drink into a rocks glass filled with ice (or one large cube) and garnish with an expressed orange twist.

ESSENTIAL 3-INGREDIENT COCKTAILS

CORPSE REVIVER NO. 1

1½ ounces Cognac

¾ ounce Calvados

¾ ounce sweet
vermouth

Orange twist,
for garnish

Corpse revivers are a series of classic cocktails meant to "revive" a person who indulged in a few too many cocktails the previous evening. The corpse reviver no. 1 first appeared in Harry Craddock's famous The Savoy Cocktail Book, *with the note, "To be taken before 11am, or whenever steam and energy are needed." The corpse reviver no. 1 is a strong, spirit-forward blend of Cognac, Calvados, and sweet vermouth. While I thoroughly enjoy this category of classic cocktails, I prefer them served in the evening or as nightcaps.*

INSTRUCTIONS:

Combine the Cognac, Calvados, and vermouth in a mixing glass. Fill ¾ of the glass with ice. Stir until chilled, about 30 seconds. Strain into a coupe glass and garnish with an expressed orange twist.

THE ORIGINS OF COGNAC

Cognac is a type of brandy made from fermented grapes in the Cognac region of France. In the 17th century, Dutch merchants were the first to make brandy from the wines in this region, and they eventually set up distilleries there. The grapes in the area made for an exceptional-tasting brandy, and the French people soon began distilling and exporting it themselves.

The benefits of long-term aging of Cognac were discovered in the early 1700s, following the end of the Spanish War of Succession. Barrels of brandy destined for England had been inadvertently stored for 12 years during the war, imparting a superior smoothness and a richness of flavor. Cognac became more and more refined, and production grew steadily until 1875 when phylloxera, a small grapevine-loving insect, destroyed nearly all of France's grapes. The infestation devastated wine and Cognac production in France, and it took decades for the industry to recover. Today, Cognac production is stable and international popularity of the spirit is on the rise, with 98 percent of Cognac being exported to countries such as the United States and China.

JAPANESE COCKTAIL

2 ounces Cognac

½ ounce orgeat

2 dashes
Angostura bitters

Lemon twist,
for garnish

The Japanese cocktail was first mentioned in the classic 1862 book How to Mix Drinks *by Jerry Thomas. It's unclear how this cocktail came to be named, as none of the ingredients are Japanese, but it has nevertheless endured. Orgeat's rich and creamy almond flavor enhances the toasted, nutty flavors of the Cognac, and an expressed lemon peel lightens and brightens the cocktail.*

INSTRUCTIONS:

Put the Cognac, orgeat, and bitters in a cocktail shaker. Fill ¾ of the shaker with ice. Shake until chilled, about 12 seconds. Strain the drink into a coupe glass and garnish with an expressed lemon twist.

ESSENTIAL 3-INGREDIENT COCKTAILS

COGNAC AND GINGER

1½ ounces Cognac

½ ounce lime juice

4 ounces ginger ale

Lime slice,
for garnish

Most cocktails featuring Cognac are bold and spirituous, but they can be light and refreshing, too. Cognac pairs beautifully with the crisp taste of ginger ale, allowing the flavor of the spirit to hold its own. A squeeze of lime juice cuts through the sweetness and makes for a very balanced, fresh afternoon sipper. Replace the soda with ginger beer for a spicier variation.

INSTRUCTIONS:

Fill a highball glass with ice. Add the Cognac and lime juice and stir to combine. Top with the ginger ale and garnish with a lime slice.

BONUS COCKTAILS

JACK ROSE

2 ounces applejack
brandy or Calvados

¾ ounce lime juice

½ ounce grenadine

Lime twist,
for garnish

The Jack Rose was invented sometime in the early 1900s and became very popular in the 1920s and 1930s. The cocktail is traditionally made with applejack brandy (such as Laird's), grenadine, and either lemon or lime juice. Applejack is made from apples and is sometimes blended with neutral grain spirits. The Jack Rose cocktail is often associated with the literary world, having been mentioned in an Ernest Hemingway novel and reportedly being the preferred cocktail of author John Steinbeck.

INSTRUCTIONS:

Put the applejack brandy, lime juice, and grenadine in a cocktail shaker. Fill ¾ of the shaker with ice. Shake until chilled, about 12 seconds. Strain the drink into a coupe glass and garnish with an expressed lime twist.

ESSENTIAL 3-INGREDIENT COCKTAILS

CHAMPAGNE COCKTAIL

1 sugar cube

2 dashes
Angostura bitters

4 ounces
Champagne

Lemon twist,
for garnish

The Champagne cocktail is among the oldest classic cocktails. A touch of sugar, aromatic bitters, and an expressed lemon twist add depth and complexity to an otherwise ordinary glass of Champagne. The sugar cube adds gradual sweetness and also increases carbonation, creating an even more effervescent glass of bubbly. If you enjoy Champagne cocktails, try swapping in different bitters, such as Peychaud's or orange, for a custom experience.

INSTRUCTIONS:

Chill a Champagne flute in the freezer at least 30 minutes before serving. Saturate a sugar cube with bitters and drop it into the chilled flute. Top with the chilled Champagne and garnish with a lemon twist.

GRASSHOPPER

1 ounce crème
de menthe

1 ounce crème
de cacao

1 ounce cream

Mint leaf,
for garnish

*The grasshopper is the quintessential
dessert drink, made with sweet mint
and chocolate liqueurs mixed with
luscious cream. Green crème de
menthe is the preferred liqueur, giving
the cocktail its signature hue. A New
Orleans bar named Tujague's lays
claim to the cocktail's origin, asserting
that the drink was invented in the
1910s by then-owner Philibert Guichet.
The grasshopper reached its peak
popularity during the 1950s and 1960s.*

INSTRUCTIONS:

Put the liqueurs and the cream in a
cocktail shaker. Fill ¾ of the shaker
with ice. Shake until chilled, about
12 seconds. Strain the drink into a
martini glass and garnish with a
mint leaf.

ESSENTIAL 3-INGREDIENT COCKTAILS

AMERICANO

1½ ounces Campari

1½ ounces sweet
vermouth

2½ ounces
sparkling water

Orange slice,
for garnish

The Americano originated in Italy in the mid-1800s as the Milano-Torino. The drink apparently became very popular with American tourists, leading to its modern-day name. If you're new to Campari, the Americano is a great introduction. The bold, bracingly bitter flavor of the red liqueur can be overwhelming, but it's softened considerably in this bubbly highball.

INSTRUCTIONS:

Fill a highball glass with ice. Add the Campari and vermouth and stir to combine. Top with the sparkling water and garnish with an orange slice.

NEGRONI SBAGLIATO

1 ounce Campari

1 ounce sweet
vermouth

1 ounce prosecco

Orange slice,
for garnish

Literally meaning "messed up Negroni," the Negroni sbagliato was reportedly invented when a bartender accidentally added sparkling wine, rather than gin, to the classic cocktail. The result was an effervescent, lighter Negroni (page 62). Not as light as an Americano, but not as strong as a classic Negroni, the Negroni sbagliato is a great alternative for those seeking a slightly less potent version. Sparkling wine also adds a festive flair to the cocktail, making it a fun celebratory cocktail for parties or occasions like New Year's Eve.

INSTRUCTIONS:

Fill a rocks glass with ice. Add the Campari and vermouth and stir to combine. Top with the prosecco and garnish with an orange slice.

ESSENTIAL 3-INGREDIENT COCKTAILS

NEGRONI SBAGLIATO, PAGE 132

APEROL SPRITZ

2 ounces Aperol

3 ounces prosecco

1 ounce
sparkling water

Orange slice,
for garnish

The Aperol spritz has been popular in Italy since the 1950s, but it has become especially fashionable during the past few years. The gently bittersweet and easy-to-sip cocktail has become symbolic of the Italian aperitivo tradition. Light and citrusy, this cocktail is enjoyable any time of day. I enjoy serving this spritz alongside a charcuterie plate on summer afternoons.

INSTRUCTIONS:

Fill a wine glass with ice. Add the Aperol, prosecco, and sparkling water. Stir gently and garnish with an orange slice.

ESSENTIAL 3-INGREDIENT COCKTAILS

ELDERFLOWER SPRITZ

1 ounce elderflower
liqueur

Juice of ½ lemon

4 ounces prosecco

Lemon wheel,
for garnish

This spritz variation is one of my go-to cocktails for spring, although you can enjoy it any time of year. The elderflower spritz is floral and fruity, making it a great brunch cocktail—elderflower liqueur takes center stage, with its unique, almost lychee-like flavor. The liqueur's sweetness is brightened with a generous splash of lemon juice and fortified with prosecco or another dry sparkling wine of your choosing.

INSTRUCTIONS:

Fill a wine glass with ice. Add the liqueur and lemon juice and stir to combine. Top with the chilled prosecco and garnish with a lemon wheel.

CAIPIRINHA

½ lime

2 teaspoons sugar

2 ounces cachaça

Brazil's national cocktail is a blend of cachaça, sugar, and lime. Cachaça is made with fermented sugarcane juice, like rhum agricole, but the two spirits are very different. Cachaças tend to have grassy, vegetal, herbal, and sometimes floral flavors that work well in tropical drinks. The caipirinha appears to have evolved out of an old medicinal beverage in the Brazilian countryside and is a rustic, no-fuss cocktail that's created in and consumed from the same glass. The caipirinha is the perfect cocktail to whip up at the beach or by the pool.

INSTRUCTIONS:

Cut the lime half into wedges. Put the lime wedges and the sugar in a double rocks glass and muddle thoroughly. Fill the glass with ice, top with the cachaça, and stir to chill.

ESSENTIAL 3-INGREDIENT COCKTAILS

ADONIS

1½ ounces dry sherry

1½ ounces sweet
vermouth

2 dashes
orange bitters

Orange twist,
for garnish

The Adonis is a light, low-ABV cocktail that has been around since the late 1800s when it was named after a popular Broadway musical. Equal parts dry sherry, such as fino, and sweet vermouth create a wonderful pre-dinner drink. The Adonis is a great cocktail for sherry lovers or those interested in classic lower alcohol cocktails.

INSTRUCTIONS:

Combine the sherry, vermouth, and bitters in a mixing glass. Fill ¾ of the glass with ice. Stir until chilled, about 30 seconds. Strain the drink into a coupe glass and garnish with an expressed orange twist.

BONUS COCKTAILS

CHRYSANTHEMUM

¼ ounce absinthe

2 ounces dry
vermouth

1 ounce Bénédictine

Orange twist,
for garnish

The chrysanthemum was first mentioned in 1916 in Hugo Ensslin's cocktail book Recipes for Mixed Drinks. *This low-ABV classic cocktail is herbal and complex, combining dry vermouth with the unique flavors of Bénédictine liqueur and a hint of anise-y absinthe. Bénédictine is an interesting herbal liqueur that is flavored with 27 botanicals including lemon balm, angelica, and hyssop.*

INSTRUCTIONS:

Put the absinthe in a coupe glass and swirl it to coat the glass. Discard the absinthe and set the glass aside. Combine the dry vermouth and Bénédictine in a mixing glass. Fill ¾ of the glass with ice. Stir until chilled, about 30 seconds. Strain the drink into the absinthe-rinsed coupe glass and garnish with an expressed orange twist.

ESSENTIAL 3-INGREDIENT COCKTAILS

SHERRY COBBLER

2 orange slices

¼ ounce simple syrup (see page 30)

3 ounces dry sherry

Mint, for garnish

Fresh fruit, for garnish

The sherry cobbler is said to have been invented in America around the mid-19th century. Interestingly, it's the cobbler, with its mound of crushed ice, that allegedly popularized the paper drinking straw. Using a straw allowed the drinker to enjoy the cocktail until the very last sip and to consume the drink more quickly. In addition to sherry, cobblers can be made with other fortified wines, such as vermouth, or even spirits.

INSTRUCTIONS:

In a cocktail shaker, muddle the orange slices with simple syrup. Add the sherry and fill ¾ of the shaker with ice. Shake until chilled, about 12 seconds. Strain the drink into a double rocks glass filled with crushed ice and top with a small mound of crushed ice. Garnish with mint and fresh fruit and serve with a straw.

TINTO DE VERANO

3 ounces red wine

3 ounces
lemon-lime soda

1 ounce
sparkling water

Lemon wheel,
for garnish

Tinto de verano *means "red wine of summer" and is also the name of one of the most popular summertime cocktails in Spain. In cities and touristy areas, it's common for locals to opt for the simple tinto de verano over much more expensive sangrias. Traditionally, tinto de verano is made with equal parts red table wine and a carbonated, lightly sweetened citrus soda. In the United States, it can be difficult to find a lightly sweetened citrus soda, so I opt for equal parts wine and soda, with a splash of sparkling water. The result is an easy-to-drink, lower-alcohol cocktail that's perfect for an outdoor picnic.*

INSTRUCTIONS:

Fill a highball glass with ice. Add the wine, soda, and sparkling water. Stir gently and garnish with a lemon wheel.

ESSENTIAL 3-INGREDIENT COCKTAILS

NORDIC SUMMER

2 ounces aquavit

1 ounce Aperol

1 ounce lime juice

Orange twist,
for garnish

This unexpected combination of aquavit, Aperol, and lime is crisp, fruity, and herbal, making it a fun happy hour option for the imbiber in search of something different. Aquavit is a clear spirit produced in Scandinavian countries and flavored with a variety of botanicals, including caraway and citrus peels. It has a unique herbal flavor that works particularly well in cocktails with citrus, such as lime or grapefruit, and vegetables, such as cucumber.

INSTRUCTIONS:

Put the aquavit, Aperol, and lime juice in a cocktail shaker. Fill ¾ of the shaker with ice. Shake until chilled, about 12 seconds. Strain the drink into a coupe glass and garnish with an expressed orange twist.

BONUS COCKTAILS

RASPBERRY RICKEY (MOCKTAIL)

8 raspberries

1½ ounces lime juice

6 ounces
sparkling water

Raspberries,
for garnish

Sometimes I want a high-quality crafted drink without the booze or sugar. This nonalcoholic, low-calorie rickey is tart and refreshing, with only a mild sweetness from the fresh raspberries. This simple mocktail can be made with any combination of berries for a custom summer refresher. To turn this mocktail into a cocktail, add 11/2 ounces of the spirit of your choice—it's great with gin or even aquavit.

INSTRUCTIONS:

Muddle the raspberries in a cocktail shaker. Add the lime juice and 1 ounce of plain water. Fill ¾ of the shaker with ice. Shake until chilled, about 12 seconds. Fine strain the drink into a highball glass filled with ice and top with the sparkling water. Garnish with raspberries on a cocktail pick and serve with a straw.

MEASUREMENT CONVERSIONS

VOLUME EQUIVALENTS (LIQUID)

US STANDARD	US STANDARD (OUNCES)	METRIC (APPROXIMATE)
2 tablespoons	1 fl. oz.	30 mL
¼ cup	2 fl. oz.	60 mL
½ cup	4 fl. oz.	120 mL
1 cup	8 fl. oz.	240 mL
1½ cups	12 fl. oz.	355 mL
2 cups or 1 pint	16 fl. oz.	475 mL
4 cups or 1 quart	32 fl. oz.	1 L
1 gallon	128 fl. oz.	4 L

VOLUME EQUIVALENTS (DRY)

US STANDARD	METRIC (APPROXIMATE)
⅛ teaspoon	0.5 mL
¼ teaspoon	1 mL
½ teaspoon	2 mL
¾ teaspoon	4 mL
1 teaspoon	5 mL
1 tablespoon	15 mL
1 cup	235 mL

WEIGHT EQUIVALENTS

US STANDARD	METRIC (APPROXIMATE)
½ ounce	15 g
1 ounce	30 g
2 ounces	60 g
4 ounces	115 g
8 ounces	225 g
12 ounces	340 g
16 ounces or 1 pound	455 g

REFERENCES

Arizona Biltmore. "Arizona Biltmore Original Tequila Sunrise." Accessed January 17, 2020. ArizonaBiltmore .com/wp-content/uploads/2016/05 /Better-Bar-Menu -2016-v6.pdf.

Blue, Anthony Dias. *The Complete Book of Spirits*. New York: HarperCollins, 2004.

Craddock, Harry. *The Savoy Cocktail Book*. 1930. Reprint, Mansfield Centre: Martino Publishing, 2015.

Difford, Simon. "Daiquiri: History and Story of its Creation." Difford's Guide. Accessed January 17, 2020. DiffordsGuide.com /g/1083/daiquiri-cocktail/story.

Embury, David A. *The Fine Art of Mixing Drinks*. 1948. Reprint, New York: Mud Puddle Books, 2008.

Encyclopedia Britannica. "Rum." Last modified November 3, 2016. Britannica.com/topic/rum-liquor.

Ensslin, Hugo. *Recipes for Mixed Drinks*. 1916. Reprint, New York: Mud Puddle Books, 2009.

Gately, Iain. *Drink: A Cultural History of Alcohol*. New York: Gotham Books, 2009.

Gosling's Rum. "Dark 'n Stormy." Accessed January 17, 2020. GoslingsRum.com/cocktails/dark-n-stormy-cocktail.

Haigh, Ted. "History Lesson: The Gin Rickey." *Imbibe*. June 24, 2009. ImbibeMagazine.com/origins-of-the -gin-rickey.

Jenkins, Moses. *A Short History of Gin*. Oxford: Shire Publications, 2019.

Kellerman, Aliza. "The Mystery Behind Who Really Created the Margarita." VinePair. Accessed January 17, 2020. VinePair.com/wine-blog/the-mystery-behind-who -really-created-the-margarita.

Petraske, Sasha and Georgette Moger-Petraske. *Regarding Cocktails*. New York: Phaidon Press, 2016.

Regan, Gary and Mardee Haidin Regan. *The Book of Bourbon*. Boston: Houghton Mifflin, 1995.

Regan, Gary. "Behind the Drink: The Moscow Mule." Liquor.com. August 22, 2011. Liquor.com/articles /behind-the-drink-the-moscow-mule/#gs.syvy2k.

Thomas, Jerry. *How to Mix Drinks*. 1862. Reprint, Kansas City: Andrews McMeel Publishing, 2015.

Wondrich, David. *Imbibe!* New York: Perigee, 2015.

INDEX

ABOUT THE AUTHOR

Amy Traynor is an award-winning cocktail blogger and photographer. Her blog, *Moody Mixologist*, was the recipient of the 2018 SAVEUR Best Drinks Blog Award. She holds a BFA in photography from the School of Visual Arts in New York City. Her photography has been exhibited internationally and featured in several publications, including *Story Gourmet*. Amy resides in New Hampshire with her husband and daughter.

CPSIA information can be obtained
at www.ICGtesting.com
Printed in the USA
JSHW021108061020
8474JS00006B/14

9 781646 118595